I0067142

Bookkeeping
in About an Hour

by Jay Butler and
Dr. Robert Hagopian

AssetProtectionServices.com

ISBN 978-0-9914644-0-1

© 2004 - 2016 Asset Protection Services of America. All Rights Reserved. AssetProtectionServices.com

BOOKKEEPING IN ABOUT AN HOUR

THE EASY AND PRACTICAL SYSTEM

Table of **Contents**

© 2004 - 2016 Asset Protection Services of America. All Rights Reserved. AssetProtectionServices.com

Disclaimer

The publication is copyrighted © 2016 by Asset Protection Services of America (hereinafter "APSA") with all rights reserved. No part of this publication may be reproduced, retransmitted or rebroadcast in any form or by any means without the express prior written consent of the copyright holder.

Information contained in this publication has been prepared for continuing research and, although these materials may be technical in nature, carries no weight other than being educational in purpose. The materials are provided only as a starting point in order for the reader to undertake his or her own investigation of the subject matter contained herein.

This publication has been garnered from sources deemed reliable at the time of rendering. Since laws, rules, rulings, regulations, statutes and codes are constantly changing and evolving, the information may not be current and APSA takes no responsibility for updating, omitting or correcting any information in this publication.

APSA offers no guarantees the information in this book as being comprehensive, exhaustive, accurate or complete and furthers the information provided is on an "AS IS" basis. Any guidance or reliance on the content found in this publication is at the sole risk of the user. APSA offers no assurances as to the suitability of any particular service or strategy meeting any stated aims, goals or objectives. APSA strongly recommends the reader seek independent accounting, financial, investing, legal, tax or other professional advice.

No representations or warranties are given or implied to render any accounting, financial, investing, legal, tax or other professional advice. No accounting, financial, investing, legal, tax or other professional advice is intended, approved or authorized by APSA. If any accounting, financial, investing, legal, tax or other professional advice is required, then a competent professional should be sought.

APSA and any APSA advisors, directors, employees, members, officers, partners, professional agencies, professional intermediaries, shareholders, staff, ultimate beneficial owners and any other affiliated firms or third-parties wherever situated, take no responsibility whatsoever, whether individually or collectively, for the manner in which the reader may choose to interpret or use the information presented in this publication. APSA shall not be held liable for any civil or criminal liability or damages whether direct, indirect, special or consequential resulting from any interpretations or use of the information provided in this publication.

This publication shall not be taken as sanctioning or advocating any unlawful act or for any improper use of any entity structure, asset protection, tax strategy or estate planning activity, nor for any illegal or fraudulent purposes.

© 2004 - 2016 Asset Protection Services of America. All Rights Reserved. AssetProtectionServices.com

Foreword

ESTILL
&
LONG, LLC
ATTORNEYS & COUNSELORS AT LAW

Scott M. Estill, Esq.
Stephanie F. Long, Esq.

2579 W. Main Street
Suite 201
Littleton, CO 80120

Office: (720) 922-1120
Fax: (720) 922-2925
www.estillandlong.com

September 3, 2013

TO WHOM IT MAY CONCERN

I have been admitted to practice law since 1988 and have spent the vast majority of this time in the tax law arena, both as an attorney for the Internal Revenue Service (1991-1995) and taxpayers (1995 to present) alike. While there are many different tax issues involved for anyone with a business, nearly all start with the adequacy and completeness of the records kept for the business. Nearly every business in the United States will overpay their taxes, year in and year out, without a proper record-keeping system in place. Without proper records, tax deductions and credits will be missed, resulting in a higher tax bill. If this isn't bad enough, if the business is "lucky" enough to be selected for a tax audit, the lack of appropriate and necessary records will result in the loss of many tax deductions claimed on the tax return, again resulting in higher overall tax bills.

In order to avoid some of these major tax problems, I recommend to my clients and at conferences/seminars where I teach that all business owners operate their business in a "businesslike" manner. This is probably the most important way to avoid overpaying taxes every year and may also avoid an audit, or at a minimum will permit a successful fight in the event of a federal or state tax audit. What a "businesslike manner" means is that the business owner should get advice before beginning the business concerning an appropriate accounting system, and should keep accurate books and records with proof of expenses while the business is in existence. This means having an actual accounting system in place. All accounting systems require the business owner to keep financial records within certain generally accepted accounting standards. Records are thus critical in order to maintain accurate financial reporting. *Bookkeeping in about an Hour* provides one "tried and true" method of gathering the applicable documents, receipts and other information to preserve, claim and be able to back up tax deductions and credits reported on your business tax return. Without these records, your accounting system will be set up to fail. By using *Bookkeeping in about an Hour*, you will be on your way to having complete tax records so that missed expenses and tax deductions will be a thing of the past!

Scott M. Estill
Attorney & Counselor at Law

© 2004 - 2016 Asset Protection Services of America. All Rights Reserved. AssetProtectionServices.com

Asset Protection Services of America

The inverted "V" displayed on our shield is the uppercase letter "L" in ancient Greek identifying the people of Lacedaemonia, which in historical times was the proper name for the Spartan state. The Greek cry "Molõn Labé" means "Come and Get Them" as spoken by King Leonidas in response to the Persian army's demand for the outnumbered Spartans (300 against 300,000) to surrender their weapons during battle in the narrow pass or 'hot gates' of Thermopylae in 480 B.C. The iconic expression has become a symbol of courage to defend that which belongs to you, even if faced against overwhelming or insurmountable odds.

Author

Jay Butler is the Managing Director of Asset Protection Services of America, the former Managing Director of Asset Protection Services International, Ltd and the former Vice-President of Sales and Marketing for Corporate Support Services of Nevada Inc. Mr. Butler holds a Bachelor's Degree of Fine Arts from Boston University.

Jay has provided customized business entity structuring for clients in all 50 states along with some of the most respected names in the industry including the Jay Mitton organization "the father of asset protection" and Real Estate Investor Association seminars.

While working with Wealth Protection Concepts, LLC under the tutelage of the former Las Vegas and North Las Vegas city attorney Carl E. Lovell Jr. (now deceased from Leukemia), Mr. Butler was bestowed the title of "Asset Protection Planner" for his competency and experience. He also co-authored the first edition of his book "Cover Your Assets: Legal Authorities on Asset Protection, Tax Strategies and Estate Planning" © 2006 with Dr. Lovell.

While residing in Switzerland, Mr. Butler was the Associate Director of "CO-Handelszentrum GmbH" providing Swiss company formation and administration services and executed a full-range of fiduciary responsibilities including sales, client support and international corporate compliance services (KYC, FATCA, AML, FATF and Swiss Code of Obligations).

Jay builds his relationships through consistent attention to detail and reliable support. He has traveled extensively throughout the United States (having visited 49 of the 50 states), explored 36 nations worldwide, and has lived in a total of 7 countries throughout North America, Central America, the Middle East, North Africa and Europe.

© 2004 - 2016 Asset Protection Services of America. All Rights Reserved. AssetProtectionServices.com

Dr Robert Hagopian is semi-retired and the former CEO of Nevada Trustee Services Group Inc, which has provided trustee services to attorneys and law firms throughout the United States since 2005, and the former CEO of the Commerce Bank Ltd in Hong Kong.

Since 1968, Robert has traveled extensively throughout Asia and lived in Japan, Hong Kong and the Philippines with current residency and offices in Manilla.

Dr. Hagopian holds a Bachelor of Science (BS) degree in business administration, an MsD (doctorate) in philosophy and a "jure Dignitatis" Bachelor of Laws degree.

Since 1984, Dr. Hagopian has been structuring business entities for optimum wealth preservation, profitability, asset protection and limiting personal liability through the use of domestic corporations, limited liability companies and various trust vehicles.

Robert has developed innovative processes for the acquisition, holding and marketing of real property. In 2008, Dr. Hagopian applied for the patent-pending "Equity Recovery Program". Based on IRC 351 rules for the transference of real estate to a corporation, the program lawfully avoids capital gains tax, self-employment and state taxes upon the sale of real property.

Contact Us

Please browse our website at www.AssetProtectionServices.com and contact us to schedule your free private asset protection consultation. We welcome the opportunity to hold a 3-way conference call with your tax advisor and/or legal counsel to address any specific questions or concerns you may have. Experience has demonstrated it favorable to have all related parties "on the same page" when creating your structure.

Asset Protection Services of America
701 South Carson Street (Suite #200)
Carson City, Nevada 89701-5239
Office   (775) 461-5255
Skype   Jay_Butler
E-Mail   info@AssetProtectionServices.com
Website www.AssetProtectionServices.com

© 2004 - 2016 Asset Protection Services of America. All Rights Reserved. AssetProtectionServices.com

Books by Jay Butler and Dr. Robert Hagopian

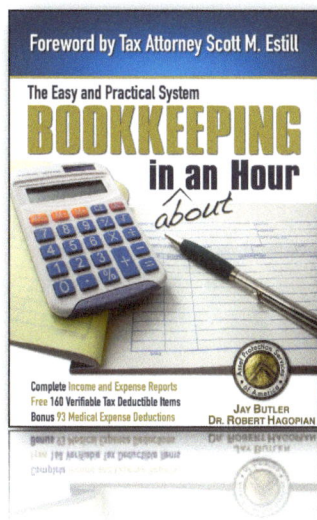
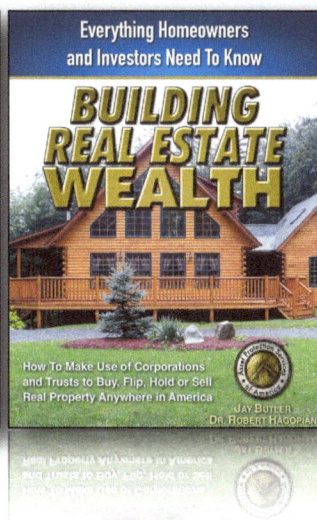
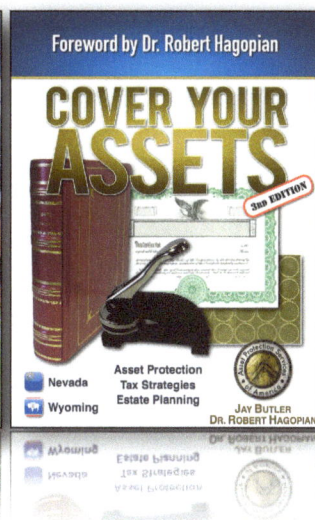
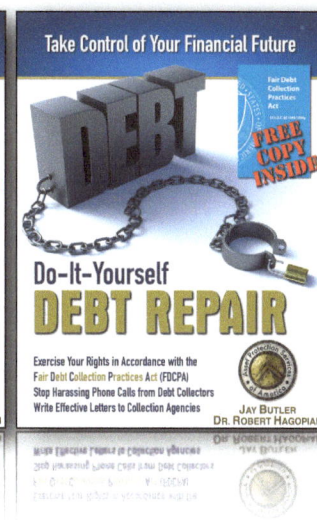

Bookkeeping in About an Hour	ISBN 978-0-9914644-0-1
Building Real Estate Wealth	ISBN 978-0-9914644-1-8
Cover Your Assets *(3rd Edition)*	ISBN 978-0-9914644-2-5
Do-It-Yourself Debt Repair	ISBN 978-0-9914644-7-0

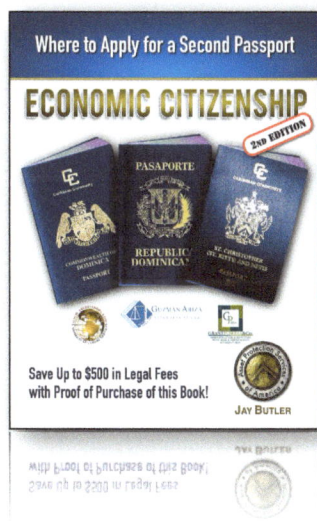
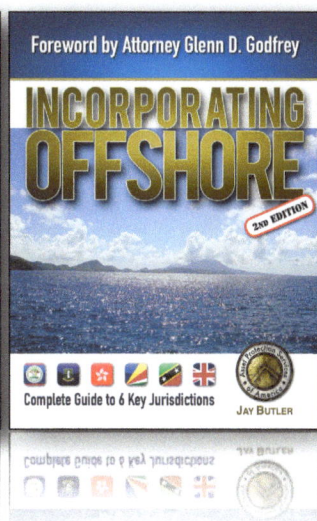
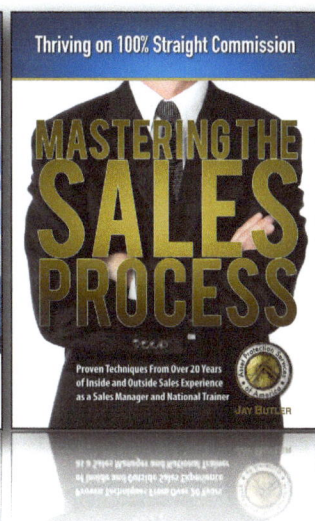
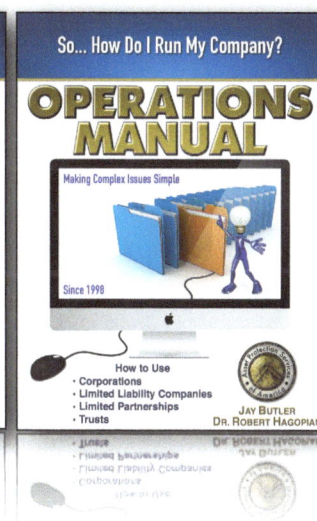

Economic Citizenship *(2nd Edition)*	ISBN 978-0-9914644-4-9
Incorporating Offshore *(2nd Edition)*	ISBN 978-0-9914644-5-6
Mastering the Sales Process	ISBN 978-0-9914644-6-3
Operations Manual	ISBN 978-0-9914644-3-2

© 2004 - 2016 Asset Protection Services of America. All Rights Reserved. AssetProtectionServices.com

Income & Expense Forms

The following forms are based on the Internal Revenue Service (IRS) Publication 535 for business expenditures. These forms are designed to provide you with the basic accounting and bookkeeping reports needed to prepare a tax return for most any type of small business.

Place all your receipts throughout the month into an envelope or folder along with your bank and credit card statements.

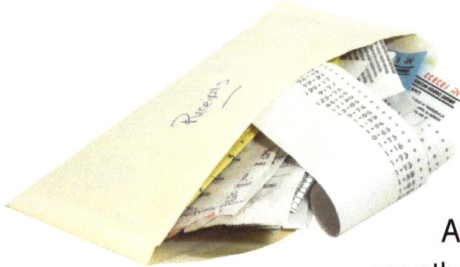

Using that information, complete the following forms (and applicable attachments) at the end of every month.

At the end of the year, take all the forms from the previous 12 months and create a year-end report for your accountant or tax preparer and title it "Annual Income & Expense Report for the Year 20____."

Your enrolled agent, CPA or tax attorney will then be able to properly and efficiently prepare your state and federal tax returns based on the accurate information you have provided.

Deductions

If you're not sure which receipts to keep on a regular basis, be sure to carefully review our Tax Deductible Items and Medical Expense Deductions listed at the end of this publication.

Per-Diem Forms

‣ A Per Diem is a flat amount of money paid and not an itemized reimbursement program.

‣ Per Diems are not allowable for 1099 Independent Contractors.

‣ Traveling Per Diem amounts vary from city to city and/or from state to state.

‣ In general, a rate of $40.00 per day has proven to be an acceptable Per Diem rate for owners and authorized employees who work past 18:00 hours (6 PM) on any weekday or over 4 hours on a weekend (while working on company premises), or when traveling more than 20 miles from the company office.

‣ Be cautious not to take 'unreasonable' advantage of Per Diems or you may invoke an IRS audit even if you qualify for the Per Diem allowance on a daily basis.

‣ Experience has shown the maximum number of Per Diem days should not exceed 2-3 days per week.

‣ For more information on IRS approved per diem rates see IRS Publication 1542.

© 2004 - 2016 Asset Protection Services of America. All Rights Reserved. AssetProtectionServices.com

Income & Expenses

*The codes in **Blue** are designed to assist your accountant or tax preparer to enter your data.*

Income (1000)

Total Monthly Income for _____, 20____ $_____

Office Expenses (2000)

Office Expenses, whether purchased or leased, requires an itemization on Exhibit "A".
If the square feet is used for a home office, then only the percentage shown can be deducted.

Code	Business	Details	Amount
2110	**Home Owners**	*Association Dues*	$_____
2120	**Insurance**	*Business Related*	$_____
2130	**Mortgage**	*Only square feet used for home office*	$_____
2140	**Rent**	*or only if for business / commercial*	$_____

Code	Communications	*Only the Percent Used for Business*	Amount
2210	**Fax**	_____	$_____
2220	**Internet**	_____	$_____
2230	**Land Line**	_____	$_____
2240	**Mobile**	_____	$_____

Code	Improvements	*Only the Percent Used for Business*	Amount
2310	**Carpeting / Flooring**	_____	$_____
2320	**Furniture**	*Requires an Itemization (See Exhibit "A")*	$_____
2330	**Lighting Fixtures**	_____	$_____
2340	**Maintenance**	_____	$_____
2350	**Meals / Food**	*Only for Employees & Clients on Premise*	$_____
2360	**Remodeling**	_____	$_____

Code	Utilities	*Only the Percent Used for Business*	Amount
2410	**Electricity**	_____	$_____
2420	**Garbage**	_____	$_____
2430	**Gas**	_____	$_____
2440	**Water**	_____	$_____

© 2004 - 2016 Asset Protection Services of America. All Rights Reserved. AssetProtectionServices.com

Expenses (2000)

Office Expenses, whether purchased or leased, requires an itemization on Exhibit "A".
If the square feet is used for a home office, then only the percentage used can be deducted.

Continued...

Code	Other	Details	Amount
2510	_____	_____	$_____
2511	_____	_____	$_____
2512	_____	_____	$_____
2513	_____	_____	$_____
2514	_____	_____	$_____
2515	_____	_____	$_____
2516	_____	_____	$_____
2517	_____	_____	$_____
2518	_____	_____	$_____
2519	_____	_____	$_____

TOTAL   Office Expenses (2000) $_____

Exhibit "A"
(Furniture Itemization)

Code	Date Purchased	Details	Amount
2320	____ / _____ / 20____	_____	$_____
2321	____ / _____ / 20____	_____	$_____
2322	____ / _____ / 20____	_____	$_____
2323	____ / _____ / 20____	_____	$_____
2324	____ / _____ / 20____	_____	$_____
2325	____ / _____ / 20____	_____	$_____
2326	____ / _____ / 20____	_____	$_____
2327	____ / _____ / 20____	_____	$_____
2328	____ / _____ / 20____	_____	$_____
2329	____ / _____ / 20____	_____	$_____

© 2004 - 2016 Asset Protection Services of America. All Rights Reserved. AssetProtectionServices.com

1099 Independent Contractor, Per Diem & Salary (3000)

Per Diem Advances, Expenses and Reimbursements, require an itemization on Exhibit "B".

Code	Date of Services	1099 Independent Contractor	Amount
3110	____ / _____ / 20____	_____	$_____
3111	____ / _____ / 20____	_____	$_____
3112	____ / _____ / 20____	_____	$_____
3113	____ / _____ / 20____	_____	$_____
3114	____ / _____ / 20____	_____	$_____
3115	____ / _____ / 20____	_____	$_____
3116	____ / _____ / 20____	_____	$_____
3117	____ / _____ / 20____	_____	$_____
3118	____ / _____ / 20____	_____	$_____
3119	____ / _____ / 20____	_____	$_____

Code	Business	Details	Amount
3210	**Advances**	*Requires an Itemization (See Exhibit "B")*	$_____
3220	**Expenses**	*Requires an Itemization (See Exhibit "B")*	$_____
3230	**Per Diem**	*Requires an Itemization (See Exhibit "B")*	$_____
3240	**Reimbursements**	*Requires an Itemization (See Exhibit "B")*	$_____

Code	Date Paid	Salaries	Amount
3310	____ / _____ / 20____	_____	$_____
3311	____ / _____ / 20____	_____	$_____
3312	____ / _____ / 20____	_____	$_____
3313	____ / _____ / 20____	_____	$_____
3314	____ / _____ / 20____	_____	$_____
3315	____ / _____ / 20____	_____	$_____
3316	____ / _____ / 20____	_____	$_____
3317	____ / _____ / 20____	_____	$_____
3318	____ / _____ / 20____	_____	$_____
3319	____ / _____ / 20____	_____	$_____

TOTAL   1099 Independent Contractor, Per Diem & Salary (3000) $_____

© 2004 - 2016 Asset Protection Services of America. All Rights Reserved. AssetProtectionServices.com

Exhibit "B"
(Per Diem Advances, Expenses and Reimbursements Itemization)

Code	Date Paid	Advances	Amount
3210	____ / _____ / 20____	_____	$_____
3211	____ / _____ / 20____	_____	$_____
3212	____ / _____ / 20____	_____	$_____
3213	____ / _____ / 20____	_____	$_____
3214	____ / _____ / 20____	_____	$_____
3215	____ / _____ / 20____	_____	$_____

Code	Date Paid	Expenses	Amount
3220	____ / _____ / 20____	_____	$_____
3221	____ / _____ / 20____	_____	$_____
3222	____ / _____ / 20____	_____	$_____
3223	____ / _____ / 20____	_____	$_____
3224	____ / _____ / 20____	_____	$_____
3225	____ / _____ / 20____	_____	$_____

Code	Date Paid	Per Diem	Amount
3230	____ / _____ / 20____	_____	$_____
3231	____ / _____ / 20____	_____	$_____
3232	____ / _____ / 20____	_____	$_____
3233	____ / _____ / 20____	_____	$_____
3234	____ / _____ / 20____	_____	$_____
3235	____ / _____ / 20____	_____	$_____

Code	Date Paid	Reimbursements	Amount
3240	____ / _____ / 20____	_____	$_____
3241	____ / _____ / 20____	_____	$_____
3242	____ / _____ / 20____	_____	$_____
3243	____ / _____ / 20____	_____	$_____
3244	____ / _____ / 20____	_____	$_____
3245	____ / _____ / 20____	_____	$_____

Note Per Diem Advances, Expenses & Reimbursements mandate supporting documentation.

© 2004 - 2016 Asset Protection Services of America. All Rights Reserved. AssetProtectionServices.com

Equipment Expenses (4000)

Major Equipment Expenses over $100, whether purchased or leased, require an itemization on Exhibit "C".

Code	Business	Details	Amount
4010	**Computer Software**	*Requires an Itemization (See Exhibit "C")*	$_____
4020	**Equipment Lease**	*Requires an Itemization (See Exhibit "C")*	$_____
4030	**Equipment Purchase**	*Requires an Itemization (See Exhibit "C")*	$_____
4040	**Equipment Repair**	*Requires an Itemization (See Exhibit "C")*	$_____
4050	**Equipment Other**	*Requires an Itemization (See Exhibit "C")*	$_____
		TOTAL Equipment Expenses (4000)	$_____

Exhibit "C" Continues on the Next Page

Code	Date Paid	Computer Software	Amount
4010	____ / _____ / 20____	_____	$_____
4011	____ / _____ / 20____	_____	$_____
4012	____ / _____ / 20____	_____	$_____
4013	____ / _____ / 20____	_____	$_____
4014	____ / _____ / 20____	_____	$_____
4015	____ / _____ / 20____	_____	$_____

© 2004 - 2016 Asset Protection Services of America. All Rights Reserved. AssetProtectionServices.com

Exhibit "C"
(Major Equipment Expenses over $100 Itemization)

Code	Date Paid	Equipment Lease	Amount
4020	____ / _____ / 20____	_____	$_____
4021	____ / _____ / 20____	_____	$_____
4022	____ / _____ / 20____	_____	$_____
4023	____ / _____ / 20____	_____	$_____
4024	____ / _____ / 20____	_____	$_____
4025	____ / _____ / 20____	_____	$_____

Code	Date Paid	Equipment Purchase	Amount
4030	____ / _____ / 20____	_____	$_____
4031	____ / _____ / 20____	_____	$_____
4032	____ / _____ / 20____	_____	$_____
4033	____ / _____ / 20____	_____	$_____
4034	____ / _____ / 20____	_____	$_____
4035	____ / _____ / 20____	_____	$_____

Code	Date Paid	Equipment Repair	Amount
4040	____ / _____ / 20____	_____	$_____
4041	____ / _____ / 20____	_____	$_____
4042	____ / _____ / 20____	_____	$_____
4043	____ / _____ / 20____	_____	$_____
4044	____ / _____ / 20____	_____	$_____
4045	____ / _____ / 20____	_____	$_____

Code	Date Paid	Equipment Other	Amount
4050	____ / _____ / 20____	_____	$_____
4051	____ / _____ / 20____	_____	$_____
4052	____ / _____ / 20____	_____	$_____
4053	____ / _____ / 20____	_____	$_____
4054	____ / _____ / 20____	_____	$_____
4055	____ / _____ / 20____	_____	$_____

© 2004 - 2016 Asset Protection Services of America. All Rights Reserved. AssetProtectionServices.com

Airplane, Boat, Trailer and Vehicle Expenses (5000)

Airplane, Boat, Trailer and Vehicle, whether purchased or leased, require an itemization on Exhibit "D".

Code	Business	Details	Amount
5010	DMV Fees	*Requires an Itemization (See Exhibit "D")*	$_____
5020	Gas & Oil	*Requires an Itemization (See Exhibit "D")*	$_____
5030	Insurance	*Requires an Itemization (See Exhibit "D")*	$_____
5040	Parking Fees	*Requires an Itemization (See Exhibit "D")*	$_____
5050	Purchases	*Requires an Itemization (See Exhibit "D")*	$_____
5060	Rentals	*Requires an Itemization (See Exhibit "D")*	$_____
5070	Repairs	*Requires an Itemization (See Exhibit "D")*	$_____
5080	Tolls	*Requires an Itemization (See Exhibit "D")*	$_____
5090	Other	*Requires an Itemization (See Exhibit "D")*	$_____
	TOTAL Airplane, Boat, Trailer and Vehicle Expenses (5000)		$_____

Exhibit "D" Continues on the Next Page

Code	Date Paid	Purchases	Amount
5050	____ / _____ / 20____	_____	$_____
5051	____ / _____ / 20____	_____	$_____
5052	____ / _____ / 20____	_____	$_____
5053	____ / _____ / 20____	_____	$_____
5055	____ / _____ / 20____	_____	$_____

© 2004 - 2016 Asset Protection Services of America. All Rights Reserved. AssetProtectionServices.com

Exhibit "D"
(Airplane, Boat, Trailer and Vehicle, whether purchased or leased, Itemization)

Code	Date Paid	DMV Fees	Amount
5010	____ / _____ / 20____	_____	$_____
5011	____ / _____ / 20____	_____	$_____
5012	____ / _____ / 20____	_____	$_____
5013	____ / _____ / 20____	_____	$_____
5014	____ / _____ / 20____	_____	$_____
5015	____ / _____ / 20____	_____	$_____

Code	Date Paid	Gas & Oil	Amount
5020	____ / _____ / 20____	_____	$_____
5021	____ / _____ / 20____	_____	$_____
5022	____ / _____ / 20____	_____	$_____
5023	____ / _____ / 20____	_____	$_____
5024	____ / _____ / 20____	_____	$_____
5025	____ / _____ / 20____	_____	$_____

Code	Date Paid	Insurance	Amount
5030	____ / _____ / 20____	_____	$_____
5031	____ / _____ / 20____	_____	$_____
5032	____ / _____ / 20____	_____	$_____
5033	____ / _____ / 20____	_____	$_____
5034	____ / _____ / 20____	_____	$_____
5035	____ / _____ / 20____	_____	$_____

Code	Date Paid	Parking Fees	Amount
5040	____ / _____ / 20____	_____	$_____
5041	____ / _____ / 20____	_____	$_____
5042	____ / _____ / 20____	_____	$_____
5043	____ / _____ / 20____	_____	$_____
5044	____ / _____ / 20____	_____	$_____
5045	____ / _____ / 20____	_____	$_____

© 2004 - 2016 Asset Protection Services of America. All Rights Reserved. AssetProtectionServices.com

Exhibit "D"
(Airplane, Boat, Trailer and Vehicle, whether purchased or leased, Itemization)

Continued...

Code	Date Paid	Rentals	Amount
5060	____ / _____ / 20____	_____	$_____
5061	____ / _____ / 20____	_____	$_____
5062	____ / _____ / 20____	_____	$_____
5063	____ / _____ / 20____	_____	$_____
5064	____ / _____ / 20____	_____	$_____
5065	____ / _____ / 20____	_____	$_____

Code	Date Paid	Repairs	Amount
5070	____ / _____ / 20____	_____	$_____
5071	____ / _____ / 20____	_____	$_____
5072	____ / _____ / 20____	_____	$_____
5073	____ / _____ / 20____	_____	$_____
5074	____ / _____ / 20____	_____	$_____
5075	____ / _____ / 20____	_____	$_____

Code	Date Paid	Tolls	Amount
5080	____ / _____ / 20____	_____	$_____
5081	____ / _____ / 20____	_____	$_____
5082	____ / _____ / 20____	_____	$_____
5083	____ / _____ / 20____	_____	$_____
5084	____ / _____ / 20____	_____	$_____
5085	____ / _____ / 20____	_____	$_____

Code	Date Paid	Other	Amount
5090	____ / _____ / 20____	_____	$_____
5091	____ / _____ / 20____	_____	$_____
5092	____ / _____ / 20____	_____	$_____
5093	____ / _____ / 20____	_____	$_____
5094	____ / _____ / 20____	_____	$_____
5095	____ / _____ / 20____	_____	$_____

© 2004 - 2016 Asset Protection Services of America. All Rights Reserved. AssetProtectionServices.com

Additional Business Expenses (6000)

Medical Expenses for 'out of pocket' payments requires an itemization on Exhibit "E".
Professional Fees require an itemization on Exhibit "F".
Client and Prospect Drinks, Entertainment and Meals requires an itemization on Exhibit "G".
Loan Repayments require an itemization on Exhibit "H".
Other Business Expenses requires an itemization on Exhibit "J".

Code	Advertising	Details	Amount
6110	**Advertising Consultants**	_____	$_____
6120	**Business Cards**	_____	$_____
6130	**Coupons / Flyers / Mailers**	_____	$_____
6140	**Internet Advertising**	Email, Google, Pay-Per-Click, etc	$_____
6150	**Magazines**	_____	$_____
6160	**Printing / Photocopying**	_____	$_____
6170	**Website and Web-Hosting**	_____	$_____
6180	**Web-Master Fees**	_____	$_____

Code	Business Travel	Details	Amount
6210	**Airfare**	_____	$_____
6220	**Ground Transport**	_____	$_____
6230	**Hotels**	_____	$_____
6240	**Meals**	_____	$_____
6250	**Sea Fare**	_____	$_____

Code	Medical	*Requires an Itemization (See Exhibit "E")*	Amount
6310	**Dental Care 'Out of Pocket'**	_____	$_____
6320	**Health Care 'Out of Pocket'**	_____	$_____
6330	**Health Insurance Premiums**	_____	$_____
6340	**Medications**	_____	$_____
6350	**Vitamins 'Out of Pocket'**	_____	$_____

Code	Professional Fees	*Requires an Itemization (See Exhibit "F")*	Amount
6410	**Business Consulting Fees**	_____	$_____
6420	**Accounting / CPA Fees**	_____	$_____
6430	**Financial Planning Fees**	_____	$_____
6440	**Legal Fees**	_____	$_____

© 2004 - 2016 Asset Protection Services of America. All Rights Reserved. AssetProtectionServices.com

Code	State Fees	Details	Amount
6510	**Business License Fees**	(DBA) Doing Business As	$_____
6520	**Business License Fees**	Required DBA License Advertising	$_____
6530	**Business License Fees**	Local	$_____
6540	**Business License Fees**	State	$_____
6550	**Secretary of State Fees**	Entity Creation and Renewal Fees	$_____

Code	Taxes Paid	Details	Amount
6610	**Federal State Taxes Paid**	_____	$_____
6620	**IRS Penalties & Late Fees**	_____	$_____
6630	**Sales Taxes Paid**	_____	$_____
6640	**Sales Tax Penalties & Fees**	_____	$_____
6650	**State Taxes Paid**	_____	$_____
6660	**State Tax Penalties & Fees**	_____	$_____

Code	Miscellaneous	Details	Amount
6710	**Bank Charges & Fees**	Late / Monthly / Transaction Fees	$_____
6720	**Client and Prospect Drinks, Meals and Entertainment**		$_____
		Requires an Itemization (See Exhibit "G")	
6730	**Equipment Supplies**	_____	$_____
6740	**Finance & Interest Charges**	_____	$_____
6750	**Loan Repayments**	*Requires an Itemization (See Exhibit "H")*	$_____
6760	**Mailing & Shipping**	_____	$_____
6765	**Meeting Rooms**	_____	$_____
6770	**Moving / Relocating**	_____	$_____
6775	**Office Supplies**	_____	$_____
6780	**Office Supplies**	_____	$_____
6785	**Seminars & Workshops**	_____	$_____
6790	**Storage**	_____	$_____
6795	**Subscriptions / Club Dues**	_____	$_____

Code	Other	Details	Amount
6810	Business Expenses	*Requires an Itemization (See Exhibit "J")*	$_____

TOTAL   Additional Business Expenses (6000) $_____

© 2004 - 2016 Asset Protection Services of America. All Rights Reserved. AssetProtectionServices.com

Exhibit "E"
(Medical Expenses for 'out of pocket' payments Itemization)

Code	Date Paid	Description	Amount
6300	_____ / _____ / 20_____	_____	$_____
6301	_____ / _____ / 20_____	_____	$_____
6302	_____ / _____ / 20_____	_____	$_____
6303	_____ / _____ / 20_____	_____	$_____
6304	_____ / _____ / 20_____	_____	$_____
6305	_____ / _____ / 20_____	_____	$_____

Exhibit "F"
(Professional Fees Itemization)

Code	Date Paid	Services	Amount
6400	_____ / _____ / 20_____	_____	$_____
6401	_____ / _____ / 20_____	_____	$_____
6402	_____ / _____ / 20_____	_____	$_____
6403	_____ / _____ / 20_____	_____	$_____
6404	_____ / _____ / 20_____	_____	$_____
6405	_____ / _____ / 20_____	_____	$_____

Exhibit "G"
(Client and Prospect Drinks, Entertainment and Meals Itemization)

Code	Date Paid	Client, Reason, Location	Amount
6720	_____ / _____ / 20_____	_____	$_____
6721	_____ / _____ / 20_____	_____	$_____
6722	_____ / _____ / 20_____	_____	$_____
6723	_____ / _____ / 20_____	_____	$_____
6724	_____ / _____ / 20_____	_____	$_____
6725	_____ / _____ / 20_____	_____	$_____
6726	_____ / _____ / 20_____	_____	$_____
6727	_____ / _____ / 20_____	_____	$_____
6728	_____ / _____ / 20_____	_____	$_____
6729	_____ / _____ / 20_____	_____	$_____

© 2004 - 2016 Asset Protection Services of America. All Rights Reserved. AssetProtectionServices.com

Exhibit "H"
(Loan Repayments Itemization)

Code	Date Paid	Description	Amount
6750	____ / _____ / 20____	_____	$_____
6751	____ / _____ / 20____	_____	$_____
6752	____ / _____ / 20____	_____	$_____
6753	____ / _____ / 20____	_____	$_____
6754	____ / _____ / 20____	_____	$_____
6755	____ / _____ / 20____	_____	$_____

Exhibit "J"
(Other Business Expenses Itemization)

Code	Date Paid	Description	Amount
6810	____ / _____ / 20____	_____	$_____
6811	____ / _____ / 20____	_____	$_____
6812	____ / _____ / 20____	_____	$_____
6813	____ / _____ / 20____	_____	$_____
6814	____ / _____ / 20____	_____	$_____
6815	____ / _____ / 20____	_____	$_____
6816	____ / _____ / 20____	_____	$_____
6817	____ / _____ / 20____	_____	$_____
6818	____ / _____ / 20____	_____	$_____
6819	____ / _____ / 20____	_____	$_____
6820	____ / _____ / 20____	_____	$_____
6821	____ / _____ / 20____	_____	$_____
6822	____ / _____ / 20____	_____	$_____
6823	____ / _____ / 20____	_____	$_____
6824	____ / _____ / 20____	_____	$_____
6825	____ / _____ / 20____	_____	$_____
6826	____ / _____ / 20____	_____	$_____
6827	____ / _____ / 20____	_____	$_____
6828	____ / _____ / 20____	_____	$_____
6829	____ / _____ / 20____	_____	$_____

© 2004 - 2016 Asset Protection Services of America. All Rights Reserved. AssetProtectionServices.com

Profit or Loss Report

Income (1000)

Total Monthly Income for _____, 20_____ $_____

Expenses (2000 - 6000)

Office Expenses (2000) $_____

1099 Independent Contractor, Per Diem & Salary (3000) $_____

Equipment Expenses (4000) $_____

Airplane, Boat, Trailer and Vehicle Expenses (5000) $_____

Additional Business Expenses (6000) $_____

                                        Total Expenses $_____

                    Total _____ **Profit** _____ **Loss** $_____

© 2004 - 2016 Asset Protection Services of America. All Rights Reserved. AssetProtectionServices.com

Weekly Per Diem Record

Name _____   Title _____

	Day	Month	Year	City	State
Monday					
	Meal Rate $		Lodge Rate $		Total $
Tuesday					
	Meal Rate $		Lodge Rate $		Total $
Wednesday					
	Meal Rate $		Lodge Rate $		Total $
Thursday					
	Meal Rate $		Lodge Rate $		Total $
Friday					
	Meal Rate $		Lodge Rate $		Total $
Saturday					
	Meal Rate $		Lodge Rate $		Total $
Sunday					
	Meal Rate $		Lodge Rate $		Total $

Date Applied for Per Diem _____ / _____ / 20_____

Approved by _____   Title _____

Signature _____   Amount Paid _____

© 2004 - 2016 Asset Protection Services of America. All Rights Reserved. AssetProtectionServices.com

Company Per Diem Record

Name _____   Title _____

	Day	Month	Year	Event
Monday				
	Describe			Total $
Tuesday				
	Describe			Total $
Wednesday				
	Describe			Total $
Thursday				
	Describe			Total $
Friday				
	Describe			Total $
Saturday				
	Describe			Total $
Sunday				
	Describe			Total $

Date Applied for Per Diem ____ / _____ / 20____

Approved by _____   Title _____

Signature _____   Amount Paid _____

© 2004 - 2016 Asset Protection Services of America. All Rights Reserved. AssetProtectionServices.com

Information for Your Tax Preparer

Entity Information

Company Name _____

Type of Entity: _____ "C" Corporation   _____ "Professional" LLC

    _____ "S" Corporation   _____ "Series" LLC

    _____ "Single - Member" LLC   _____ Limited Partnership

    _____ "Multi - Member" LLC   _____ Other_____

State of Incorporation _____   Fiscal Year-End_____

Business Purpose _____

Do You File Quarterly Tax Returns?   ___ Yes ___ No

Do Your Assets Exceed $1 Million?   ___ Yes ___ No

Entity Ownership

Name of Shareholder / Member / Partner _____

Social Security Number   _____ / ____ / _____   % of Ownership _____

Employer Identification Number   _____ / ____ / _____   # of Shares / Interests _____

Name of Shareholder / Member / Partner _____

Social Security Number   _____ / ____ / _____   % of Ownership _____

Employer Identification Number   _____ / ____ / _____   # of Shares / Interests _____

Name of Shareholder / Member / Partner _____

Social Security Number   _____ / ____ / _____   % of Ownership _____

Employer Identification Number   _____ / ____ / _____   # of Shares / Interests _____

© 2004 - 2016 Asset Protection Services of America. All Rights Preserved. AssetProtectionServices.com

Asset Protection Services of America

"I live in Alexandria Virginia. Near the Supreme Court Chambers is a toll bridge across the Potomac. When in a rush, I pay the quarter toll and get home early. However, I usually drive outside the downtown section of the city and cross the Potomac on a free bridge. This bridge was placed outside the downtown Washington, DC area to serve a useful social service, getting drivers to drive the extra mile and to help alleviate congestion during rush hour. If I went over the toll bridge and through the barrier without paying the toll, I would be committing tax evasion. If, however, I drive the extra mile outside the city of Washington to the free bridge, I am using a legitimate, logical, and suitable method of tax avoidance, and I am performing a useful social service by doing so. For my tax evasion, I should be punished. For my tax avoidance, I should be commended. The tragedy of life today is that so few people know that the free bridge even exists."

Supreme Court Justice
Louis D. Brandeis
(1916-1939)

Tax Deductible Items

The following list of Tax Deductible Items may not be current, but need not be current for its intended purpose. This illustration is designed to show verifiable deductible expenditures. As with any tax advise, please seek competent counsel in your home jurisdiction.

Individual Tax Deductions

> **1.)** Home
>
> **2.)** Children
>
> **3.)** Rental Properties
>
> **4.)** Limited Business Deductions

Corporate Tax Deductions

Tax Deductible Items	Description	Standard Federal Tax Report
Abandonment of business	Real Property	¶ 9902.177
Accident and health plans	Employer contributions	¶ 8522.386
Accounting fees	Business	¶ 8520.315
	Capital transactions	¶ 13,709.01
	Connected with trade or business	¶ 8520.315
	Investors	¶ 12,523.03
	Organization of business: ($5,000 deduction, excess amortizable over 15 years)	¶ 13,352.01
Accounting system	Installation	¶ 13,709.135
Advertising expenses	Business cards	¶ 8851.133
	Catalogs long term	¶ 21,817.2075
	Generally	¶ 8851.01
	Home demonstrations	¶ 8851.1337
	Package design costs	¶ 8520.028
	Prizes and contents	¶ 8851.1657
	Product launch costs	¶ 8520.028
	Promotional activities	¶ 8851.1659
Airplane	Heavy maintenance expenses	¶ 8526.5175
Alcohol fuels credit	Unused	¶ 12,430.01

© 2004 - 2016 Asset Protection Services of America. All Rights Reserved. AssetProtectionServices.com

Tax Deductible Items	Description	Standard Federal Tax Report
Amortization of premium	On taxable bonds (Optional)	¶ 11,855.01
Appraisal fees	Connection with trade or business	¶ 8520.3152
Architect's fees	Capital expenditure	¶ 13,709.149
Architectural services	Domestic production activities	¶ 12,476.01
Attorney's and accountant's fees in contesting tax claims	Non-business	¶ 8526.462
Attorney's fees	Accounting suit by former partner, defense of	¶ 13,603.243
	Business debts, collection of	¶ 8526.429
	Civil rights suits	
	Disbarment proceedings	¶ 6005.01
	Tax advice on investments	¶ 8526.032
	Business use employee unreimbursed	¶ 12,523.346
Automobile expenses	Chauffeur's salary	¶ 8590.01
	Cost of car	¶ 8590.01
	Garage rentals	¶ 8590.033
	Gas	¶ 8590.024
	Insurance	¶ 8590.024
	License fees	¶ 8590.252
	Loss on sale	¶ 8590.024
	Oil and lubrication	¶ 8590.037
	Parking	¶ 8590.024
	Repairs	¶ 8590.024
	Tires	¶ 8590.024
	Washing	¶ 8590.024
	Rural mail carriers (limited)	¶ 8590.024
	Business	¶ 8590.022
Bad debts		¶ 10,650.021
Baseball team equipment	For business publicity	¶ 8851.184
Bookmakers	Business expenses	¶ 8521.1260
Building property	Energy efficient property for commercial buildings	¶ 12,138D.01
Building replacements	Capital expenditure	¶ 8630.51
Burglar alarm system	Cost of installing (Capital expense)	¶ 13,709.119

© 2004 - 2016 Asset Protection Services of America. All Rights Reserved. AssetProtectionServices.com

Tax Deductible Items	Description	Standard Federal Tax Report
Business conventions	Cruise ships (limited)	¶ 14,408A.059
	Foreign conventions (limited)	¶ 14,408A.0591
	Political conventions (related to trade or business)	¶ 8550.2835
	Travel expenses	¶ 8550.025, and ¶ 8550.257 to ¶ 8550.284
Business expenses	General	¶ 8520.01
Business meals	General (50%)	¶ 8523.024, ¶ 8570.0021 and ¶ 14,408A.027
Business startup expenses	($5,000 deduction, excess amortizable over 15 years)	¶ 12,371.01
Car expenses	See "automobile expenses"	¶ 14,408A.0591
Caribbean convention expenses	Business	
Carrying charges	Deductible as interest where: installment sales contract states carrying charge separately	¶ 9200.03
Casualty losses	Business	¶ 10,005.041
Charitable contributions	Corporations (limited)	¶ 11,680.021
	Computer technology, including equipment to schools, public libraries	¶ 11,680.037
	Appreciated property	¶ 11,660.04 to ¶ 11,660.047
Circulation expenditures	Newspapers, magazines, periodicals	¶ 12,032.01
Club dues	(limited)	¶ 8853.025
Coal royalty contracts	If there is no production, or no income under contracts	¶ 14,311.01
Commissions	Paid as compensation	¶ 5507.022
	Sale of real estate or securities	¶ 8521.046
	Sale of real estate or securities (dealers)	¶ 8521.049
Commissions on sale of real estate and securities	Dealer only (other than taxpayers deducting from selling price)	¶ 8521.046 and ¶ 8521.049
Compensation	Reasonable	¶ 8636.01

© 2004 - 2016 Asset Protection Services of America. All Rights Reserved. AssetProtectionServices.com

Tax Deductible Items	Description	Standard Federal Tax Report
Computer software (business use)	Development costs Leased software Purchased software	¶ 12,047.057 ¶ 12,047.115 ¶ 11,009.027 ¶ 12,047.115 ¶ 13,709.016
Construction	Domestic production activities	¶ 12,476.01
Contributions by employer to employer-financed accident and health plans	For benefit of employees	¶ 8752.01
Contributions by employer to state	State unemployment insurance and State disability funds	¶ 8752.01
Contributions paid (within certain limits)	Charitable organizations (etc.)	¶ 11,620.04 and ¶ 11,670.01
Conventions (see "Business conventions")		
Cooperative housing corporation	Share of taxes or interest paid	¶ 12,603.01 and ¶ 12,603.15
Copyright costs		¶ 11,016.021
Cost recovery	Business property or property held for the production of income	¶ 11,004.01
Cruise ships (limited)	Business conventions	¶ 14,408A.059
Custodian fees		¶ 13,709.591
Depletion		¶ 23,924.01
Depreciation	Business property or property held for the production of income Election to expense (limited)	¶ 11,004.01 ¶ 12,126.01
Disbarment proceedings	Attorney's fees & defense expenses	¶ 8526.032
Doctor's staff privilege hospital fees	Capital expenditures	¶ 13,709.323
Domestic production activities		¶ 12,476.01
Dues	Chamber of Commerce Professional associations	¶ 8853.155 ¶ 8634.102 to ¶ 8634.1142

© 2004 - 2016 Asset Protection Services of America. All Rights Reserved. AssetProtectionServices.com

Tax Deductible Items	Description	Standard Federal Tax Report
Educational assistance	Plan payments	¶ 7353.023
Efficiency engineer's fees		¶ 8520.317
Electricity	Domestic production activities	¶ 12,476.01
Embezzlement loss		¶ 10,101.024
Employee's expenses	Entertaining customers and reimbursed expenses	¶ 8524.025
	Meals and lodging away from home reimbursed	¶ 8550.021
	Move to a new work location	¶ 12,623.021
Employee's life insurance	Paid by employer (employee beneficiary)	¶ 8522.386
Employee	Severance payments to employees	¶ 8752.676
	Training expenses for employees	¶ 8572.676
	Fees for obtaining employees	¶ 8524.03
		¶ 8524.25
Employment taxes	Employer's payment under Federal Unemployment Tax Act	¶ 9502.042 and ¶ 9502.30
	Employer (but not deductible if paid on wages of domestics) Employer's taxes under Federal Insurance Contributions Act	¶ 9502.042
	Employer (deductible as a business expense) Employer's taxes under Railroad Retirement Act (deductible as a business expense)	¶ 9502.28
	Federal Unemployment Tax Act	¶ 9502.042
	Railroad Retirement Act	¶ 9502.28
	Social Security Act	¶ 9502.29
Energy efficient property	Commercial building property	¶ 12,138D.01
Engineering services	Domestic Production Activities	¶ 12,476.01
	Food furnished to employees on the premises	¶ 7438.052
	Meals directly related to business (50% deductible)	¶ 8523.024
	Meals provided for customers (50% deductible)	¶ 8523.024

© 2004 - 2016 Asset Protection Services of America. All Rights Reserved. AssetProtectionServices.com

Tax Deductible Items	Description	Standard Federal Tax Report
Environmental clean-up costs	Brownfields Hazardous waste from taxpayer's Business	¶ 12,465.01 ¶ 8630.027
Environmental impact statement	Preparation of statement	¶ 12,047.122
Environment protection agency	Sulfur regulation compliance (limited)	¶ 12,136.01
Fiduciaries fees		¶ 24,267.463
Film and television	Domestic production activities Small film & television production (limited)	¶ 12,476.01 ¶ 12,146.01
Finance charges	Other than carrying charges or loan Fees (limited)	¶ 9200.01
Fines & Penalties	Fair Labor Standards Act (awards) NLRB awards	¶ 8954.3265 ¶ 8954.3265
Firefighter	Rubber coat, helmet, boots, etc.	¶ 8524.265
Fishing boat crews (commercial)	Member's protective clothing	¶ 8524.265
Foreign conventions	(limited)	¶ 14,408A.0591
Foreign taxes (unless credit taken)	By payor	¶ 9502.032
Forfeitures (business transactions)	Advance payments Lease deposits Purchase price Interest (premature withdraw from time savings account)	¶ 9805.103 ¶ 9805.163 ¶ 9805.172 ¶ 9805.165
Fringe benefits	Cost of providing non-cash benefits	¶ 9051.01
Furnishings and fixtures	Business cost	¶ 11,279.335
Gas	Domestic production activities	¶ 12,476.01
Gifts (business)	Limited to $25 per donee per year	¶ 14,408A.038
Gifts to charity	Corporations (limited) Appreciated property	¶ 11,680.021 ¶ 11,660.04 to ¶ 11,660.047

© 2004 - 2016 Asset Protection Services of America. All Rights Reserved. AssetProtectionServices.com

Tax Deductible Items	Description	Standard Federal Tax Report
Gifts to employees	Awards for length of service (limited)	¶ 14,408A.038 ¶ 14,408A.045
	Gifts valued at $25 or less	¶ 8520.334 and ¶ 14,408A.038
Golden Parachutes	Parachute Payments	¶ 15,152.01 to ¶ 15,152.066
Golf course	Land preparation costs for greens	¶ 11,007.189
	Maintenance and operating costs	¶ 8521.124 and ¶ 8630.1292
	Employee	¶ 14,854.021
	Principal place of business	¶ 14,854.027
	Storage of product samples	¶ 14,854.021
Impairment - related work expenses	Attendant care services at work	¶ 6064.01
	Necessary expenses at work	¶ 6064.01
Import duties	(Unless as a business expense)	¶ 9502.032
Improvements by lessee	Depreciation and amortization	¶ 12,105.42
Income tax	State	¶ 9502.031
Income tax liability	Cost of determining	¶ 12,523.3844
Income tax returns	Cost of preparing (non-business)	¶ 8526.462
		¶ 12,523.3844
		¶ 12,523.44
Infringement litigation	In course of business	¶ 8526.449
Injuries to employees	Payments for (not compensated by insurance)	¶ 8752.01
Insurance expenses (business)	Casualty	¶ 8522.3815
	Malpractice	¶ 8522.392
	Insured employees or beneficiary	¶ 8522.386
	Key employees	¶ 14,008.01
	Required for credit (premiums paid by creditor)	¶ 14,008.035
Intangible assets	As defined in Code Section #197	¶ 12,455.01
Interest	(with exceptions & limitations)	¶ 9104.01
	Related to life insurance contracts	¶ 9104.048 and ¶ 14,008.021
	Property held for rent or royalty	¶ 9402.04
	Trade or business debts	¶ 9104.01
Interest forfeiture	Premature withdrawal from time savings account	¶ 9805.165

© 2004 - 2016 Asset Protection Services of America. All Rights Reserved. AssetProtectionServices.com

Tax Deductible Items	Description	Standard Federal Tax Report
Interest on tax deficiencies	Corporation	¶ 9400A.04
Investigatory costs	Business Search	¶ 12,371.25
ISO	9000 costs	¶ 8520.028 and ¶ 8520.3175
Labor union dues		¶ 8853.20
Laundry	Dry cleaning, pressing charges (business travel related)	¶ 8550.021
Legal expenses and fees	Business	¶ 8526.021 to ¶ 8526.05
	Investors	¶ 8526.4394 and ¶ 12,523.025
	Production of income	¶ 12,523.3375
	Tax determination	¶ 12,523.346
License fees		¶ 9502.398
Life insurance premiums	Debts incurred to purchase, paid by employer	¶ 8636.27
	Employee or other beneficiary	¶ 14,008.01
Lobbying expense	Professional lobbyist's expenses	¶ 8952.0664 and ¶ 8952.468
Losses	Net operating loss	¶ 12,014.01
	Sale or exchange of property (business)	¶ 9804.03
	Capital assets (business motive)	¶ 9804.03
	Rent or royalty generating property	¶ 9808.01
	Worthless stock and securities	¶ 10,001.01
Lump sum distribution	Ordinary income portion	¶ 18,217A.026
Machinery	Incidental repairs	¶ 8630.025
Materials and supplies	Business (incidentals)	¶ 8610.01
Meals provided by employees	Employer's cost of providing meals on premises	¶ 7438.052
	Meals related to business (50%)	¶ 8523.024
Medical, dental and hospital expenses	See "Medical Expense Deductions"	¶ 12,543.01
Medical insurance premiums	See "Medical Expense Deductions"	

© 2004 - 2016 Asset Protection Services of America. All Rights Reserved. AssetProtectionServices.com

Tax Deductible Items	Description	Standard Federal Tax Report
Medical savings account		¶ 12,675.01
Mine development	Expenditures	¶ 24,094.01
Mine exploration	Expenditures	¶ 24,115.01
Moving machinery		¶ 8520.50
National Labor Relations Board	Award to employees, payment by employer	¶ 8954.3265
Net operating loss deduction		¶ 12,014.01
New business, cost of start-up	($50,000 deduction and excess amortizable over 15 years)	¶ 12,371.01
Non-trade or non-business expenses	Incurred in preserving income producing Property Principal place of business	¶ 12,523.01 ¶ 14,854.027
Office supplies		¶ 8610.301
Operating loss in prior or next year		¶ 12,014.023
Organization of corporate expenses	($5,000 deduction and excess amortizable over 15 years)	¶ 13,352.01
Package design costs		¶ 8520.028
Passport fee	Business trip	¶ 9502.41
Permanent improvements	Business property Tenants	¶ 13,709.325 ¶ 12,105.42 and ¶ 13,854.035
Postage costs	Business	¶ 8610.14 and ¶ 8851.1652
Premiums paid on a business insurance	"Professional overhead expense disability policy"	¶ 8522.385
Prepaid interest or finance charges		¶ 9402.04
Prizes and contests	See "promotional activities"	
Professional association dues		

© 2004 - 2016 Asset Protection Services of America. All Rights Reserved. AssetProtectionServices.com

Tax Deductible Items	Description	Standard Federal Tax Report
Professional books and journals	Information services	
Professional activities	Coupons Prizes and contests	¶ 21,015.01 ¶ 8851.1657
Protective clothing		¶ 8524.05
Reconditioning and health - restoring	Expenses of employees (paid by employers)	¶ 8520.246
Refinery property	(limited)	¶ 12,137E.01
Reforestation costs		¶ 23,929.195
Reimbursed expenses	(Otherwise deductible)	¶ 8524.025
Removal of architectural and transportation barriers	Handicapped and elderly (limited)	¶ 12,264.01
Rent	Business Property	¶ 8754.01
Repairs	Business Property	¶ 8630.01
Research and experimental expenditures	Connected with a trade or business	¶ 12,047.01
Restaurant small wares	(limited)	¶ 8610.146
Retirement plans	Contributions to employer Individuals (limited) Self-employed individuals Simplified employee pension contributions	¶ 18,347.01 ¶ 18,922.0226 ¶ 17,933.01 ¶ 18,922.0245
Returns; Federal or state income tax, gift tax, etc.	Cost having prepared (include investor)	¶ 8520.73 and ¶ 12,523.3844
Safe deposit boxes, rental for protection of income producing property	Business use	¶ 12,523.23
Salaries	Bonuses Commissions Related Parties	¶ 8642.01 ¶ 5507.022 ¶ 8638.01
Severance payments		¶ 8752.676

© 2004 - 2016 Asset Protection Services of America. All Rights Reserved. AssetProtectionServices.com

Tax Deductible Items	Description	Standard Federal Tax Report
Shareholders proxy fight	Expenses	¶ 12,523.3593
Social security taxes	Employers (as business expense)	¶ 9502.042
Soil and water conservation	Expenditures for farmers	¶ 8756.026
Stamp taxes	Dealers / investors Trade or business	¶ 9502.032 ¶ 9502.032
Start-up business expenditures	($5,000 deduction and excess amortizable over 15 years)	¶ 12,371.01
Subscriptions, professional journals	Self-employed	¶ 6005.04
Tax refresher course	Lawyers	¶ 8632.645
Tax returns (business)	Cost of preparation	¶ 12,523.3844
Taxes	Deductible by manufacturer, producer, importer, or corresponding person, but not by consumer) Automobile excise tax	¶ 9502.01 ¶ 9502.35
Telephone service	As a business expense	¶ 8520.74
Theft loss	Business	¶ 10,101.136
Timber	Reforestation expenses ($10,000 deduction and excess amortizable over 7 years) Port-establishment fertilization	¶ 12,335.01 ¶ 8520.7455
Tires	See "automobile expenses" and "truck tires"	
Title costs (capital expenditure)	Perfecting or defending title to property, costs of defending condemnation proceedings	¶ 8526.4682 to ¶ 8526.471 and ¶ 12,523.35
Tools	Un-reimbursed cost, useful life of (one) 1 year or less	¶ 8524.04
Trade association dues	Un-reimbursed dues, reimbursed employee expenses	¶ 8853.50 to ¶ 8853.57
Trade or business	Expenses	

© 2004 - 2016 Asset Protection Services of America. All Rights Reserved. AssetProtectionServices.com

Tax Deductible Items	Description	Standard Federal Tax Report
Trade or business	Expenses	
Trademark and trade name	Expenditures	¶ 13,709.016 ¶ 31,044.055 ¶ 9502.032
Travel	Expenses reimbursed	¶ 8550.29 and ¶ 8550.48
Uniform or special clothing costs	Clothing required for business	¶ 8524.2658
Union payments	Dues Fines	¶ 8853.20 ¶ 8853.205
Wages and salaries		¶ 8636.01
Water, Potable	Domestic production activities	¶ 12,476.01

© 2004 - 2016 Asset Protection Services of America. All Rights Reserved. AssetProtectionServices.com

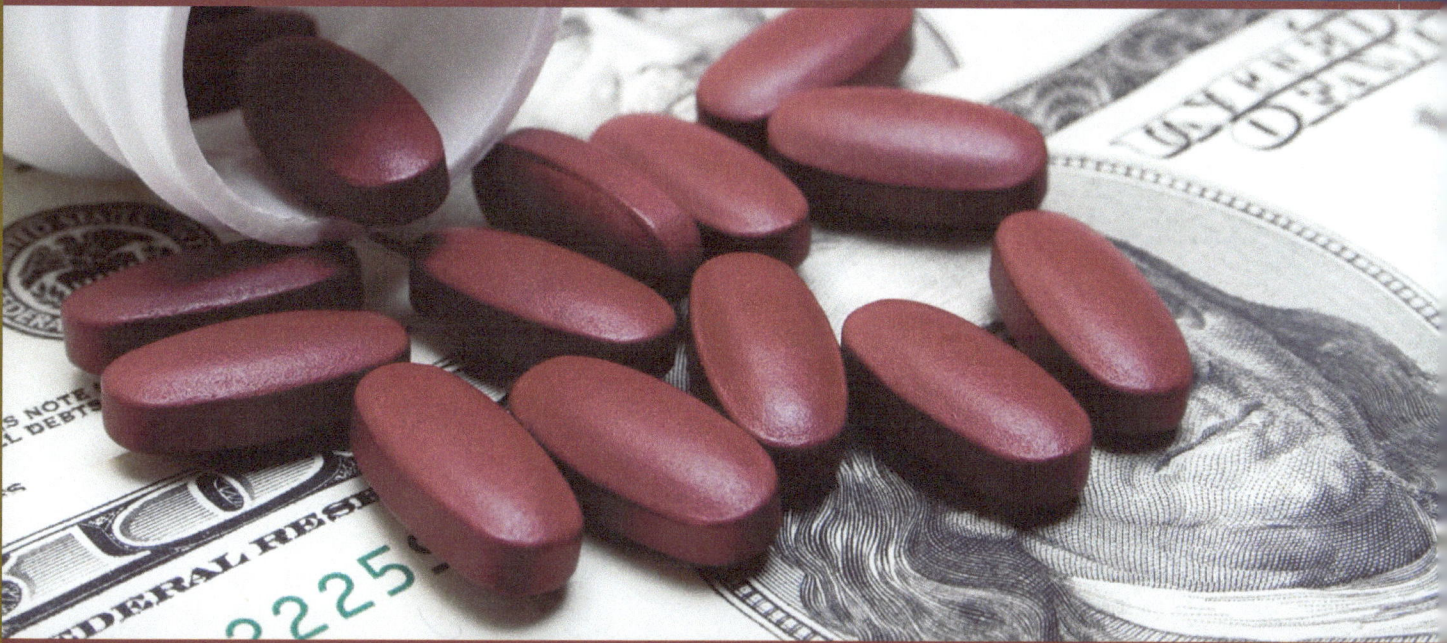

"The doctor of the future will give no medicine, but will interest his patient in the care of the human frame, in diet and in the cause and prevention of disease."

**3rd President of the U.S.
Thomas Jefferson
(1743-1826)**

AssetProtectionServices.com

Medical Expense Deductions

The following list of Medical Expense Deductions may not be current, but need not be current for its intended purpose. This illustration is designed to show verifiable deductible medical expenditures. As with any tax advise, please seek competent counsel in your home jurisdiction.

Medical Expense Deductions	Revenue Ruling / Code Section / Regulation
Abortion - legal	Rev. Rul. 73-201, 1973-1 CB 140 as clarified by Rev. Rul. 73-603, 1973-2 CB 76 Rev. Rul. 97-9, 1997-1 CB 77
Accident and health insurance - medical care separately stated and reasonable in amount	Code Sec. 213(d)(1)(C) and (d)(6) Reg. § 1.213-1(e)(4)
Acupuncture	Rev. Rul. 72-593, 1972-2 CB 180
Adoption - medical costs of adopted child	Rev. Rul. 60-255, 1960-2 CB 105
Air Conditioner - allergy relief - cystic fibrosis relief	Rev. Rul. 55-261, 1955-1 CB 307 R. Gerald, 37 TC 826, Dec. 25,331 (Acq.)
Alcoholism, treatment of	Rev. Rul. 73-325, 1973-2 CB 75
Ambulance hire	Reg. § 1.213-1 (e)(1)(ii)
Attendant to accompany blind or deaf student	Rev. Rul. 64-173, 1964-1 CB (Part 1) 121; R.A. Baer Est.26 TCM 170, Dec. 28,352(M), TC Memo. 1967-34
Birth control pills	Rev. Rul. 73-200, 1973-1 CB 140
Blind persons - attendant to accompany student	Rev. Rul. 64-173, 1964-1 (Part 1) CB 121
- braille books, magazines, excess cost of editions	Rev. Rul. 75-318, 1975-2 CB 88
- seeing eye dog	Rev. Rul. 55-261, 1955-1 CB 307
- special education (See "schools special")	
- special educational aids to mitigate condition	Rev. Rul. 58-223, 1958-1 CB 156
Capital expenditures - home modifications for handicapped individual	Rev. Rul. 87-106, 1987-2 CB 67
- primary purpose medical care	Reg. § 1.213-1(e)(1)(iii)

© 2004 - 2016 Asset Protection Services of America. All Rights Reserved. AssetProtectionServices.com

Medical Expense Deductions

Revenue Ruling / Code Section / Regulation

Medical Expense Deductions	Revenue Ruling / Code Section / Regulation
Car	
- equipped to accommodate wheelchair passage	Rev. Rul. 70-606, 1970-2 CB 66
- special controls for a person with a disability	S.H. Weinzimer, 17 TCM 712, Dec. 23,100(M), TC Memo. 1958-137
Chemical dependency treatment (see "Alcoholism treatment", "Drug addiction")	
- mother	IRS Letter Ruling 8919009
Chiropractors	Rev. Rul. 63-91, 1963-1 CB 54
Christian science treatment	Rev. Rul. 55-261, 1955-1 CB 307
Clarinet lessons, alleviation of severe teeth malocclusion	Rev. Rul. 62-210, 1962-2 CB 89
Computer data bank, storage, retrieval of medical records	Rev. Rul. 71-282, 1971-2 CB 166
Contact lenses	Reg. § 1.213-1(e)(1)(iii)
Contraceptives, prescription	Rev. Rul. 73-200, 1972-1 CB 140
Cosmetic surgery	
- ameliorate a deformity arising from congenital abnormality, personal injury, or disfiguring disease	Code Sec. 213 (d)(9); Senate Finance Committee Report to P.L. 101-508
Crutches	Reg. § 1.213-1(e)(1)(iii)
Deaf persons	
- hearing aid	Rev. Rul. 55-261, 1955-1 CB 307
- hearing aid animal	Rev. Rul. 68-295, 1968-1 CB 92
- lip reading expenses for the deaf	Rev. Rul. 55-261, 1955-1 CB 307
- notetaker, deaf student	R.A. Baer Est., 26 TCM 170, Dec. 28,352 (M), TC Memo. 1967-34
- special education (See "schools, special")	Rev. Rul. 71-48, 1971-1 CB 99, as amplified by
- telephone, specially equipped, including repairs	Rev. Rul. 73-53, 1973-1 CB 139 Rev. Rul. 80-340, 1980-2 CB 81
- television, closed caption decoder	IRS Letter Ruling 8250040, 9-13-82,
- visual alert system	CCH IRS Letter Ruling Reports
Dental fees	Reg. § 1.213-1(e)(1)(ii)
Dentures (artificial teeth)	Reg. § 1.213-1(e)(1)(ii)
Diagnostic fees	Reg. § 1.213-1 (e)(1)(ii)

© 2004 - 2016 Asset Protection Services of America. All Rights Reserved. AssetProtectionServices.com

Medical Expense Deductions	Revenue Ruling / Code Section / Regulation
Diapers, disposable used to severe neurological disease	IRS Letter Ruling 8137085, 6-17-81, CCH IRS Letter Rulings Report
Doctor's fees	Reg. § 1.213-1(e)(1)(i)
Domestic aid type that would be rendered by nurse	Rev. Rul. 58-339, 1958-2 CB 106
Drug addiction, recovery from	Rev. Rul. 72-226, 1972-1 CB 96
Drugs, prescription	Code Sec. 213(b)
Dyslexia, language training	Rev. Rul. 69-607, 1969-2 CB 40
Elevator, alleviation of cardiac condition	J.E. Berry, DC Okla., 58-2 USTC ¶ 9870, 174 Fsupp 748; Rev. Rul. 59-411, 1952-2 Cb100 as modified by Rev. Rul. 83-33, 1983-1 CB 70
Eye examinations and glasses	Reg. § 1.213-1 (e)(1)(ii),(iii)
Fertility enhancement	IRS Publication No. 502, "Medical and Dental Expenses"
Fluoride device; on advice of dentist	Rev. Rul. 64-267, 1964-2 CB 69
Glasses	Reg. § 1.213-1 (e)(1)(ii)
Halfway house, adjustment to mental hospital	IRS Letter Ruling 7714016, no date given, CCH IRS Letter Rulings Report

Handicapped persons
  (see "Specific handicap" or "Equipment")
- home modification (see "Capital expenses")
- special training or education
  (see "Schools, special")	

Health club dues - prescribed by physician for medical condition	Rev. Rul. 55-261, 1955-1 CB 307
Health Maintenance Organization (HMO)	IRS Publication No. 52, "Medical and Dental Expenses"
Hearing aids (see "Deaf persons")	
Hospital care, in-patient	Reg. § 1.213-1(e)(1)(v) hospital services Reg. § 1.213-1.e1

© 2004 - 2016 Asset Protection Services of America. All Rights Reserved. AssetProtectionServices.com

Medical Expense Deductions	**Revenue Ruling / Code Section / Regulation**
Indian medicine man	R.H. Tso, 40 TCM 1277, Dec. 37,260(M), TC Memo. 1980-339 Insulin Code Sec. 213(b)
Insurance - accident and health insurance (see "Accident and health insurance") - long term care insurance (limits) - Medicare A coverage - premium for medical care - self-employed	 Code Sec. 213(d)(1)(D); Code Sec. 7702B Rev. Rul. 79-175, 1979-1 CB 117 Reg. § 1.213-1(e)(4) Code Sec. 162(1)
Iron lung	Rev. Rul. 55-261, 1955-1 CB 307
Laboratory fees	Reg. § 1.213-1(e)(1)(ii)
Lamaze classes (see "Childbirth preparation classes")	
Laser eye surgery	Rev. Rul. 2003-57, 2003-1 CB 959
Lead paint, removal	Rev. Ru. 79-66, 1979-1 CB 114
Legal expenses - authorization of treatment for mental illness	 Rev. Rul. 71-281, 1979-2 CB 165
Lifetime medical care, prepaid; retirement home	Rev. Rul. 75-302, 1972-2 CB 86, as clarified by Rev. Rul. 93-72, 1993-2 CB 77; Rev. Rul. 75-303, 1972-2 CB 87
Limbs, artificial	Reg. § 1.213(e)(1)(ii)
Lodging (limited to $50 per night)	Code Sec. 213(d)(2)
Long term care expenses	Code Sec. 213(d)(1)(C); Code Sec. 7702B
Mattress, prescribed for alleviation of arthritis	Rev. Rul. 55-261, 1955-1 CB 307
Nursing home, medical reasons	W.B. Counts, 42 TC 755, Dec. 26,893 (Acq.)
Nursing services (including board and social security tax if paid by tax payer)	Rev. Rul. 57-489, 1957-2 CB 207
Obstetrical expenses	Reg. § 1.213-1(e)(1)(ii)
Operations - legal	Reg. § 1.213-1(e)(1)(ii)

© 2004 - 2016 Asset Protection Services of America. All Rights Reserved. AssetProtectionServices.com

Medical Expense Deductions	Revenue Ruling / Code Section / Regulation
Optometrists	Rev. Rul. 55-261, 1955-1 CB 307
Orthodontia	Reg. § 1.213-1(e)(1)(ii)
Orthopedic shoes, excess cost	IRS Letter Ruling 8221118, 2-26-82, CCH IRS Letter Ruling Reports
Osteopaths	Rev. Rul. 63-91, 1963-1 CB 54
Oxygen equipment, breathing difficulty	Rev. Rul. 55-261, 1955-1 CB 307
Patterning exercises, handicapped child	Rev. Rul. 70-170, 1970-1 CB 51
Plumbing, special fixtures for handicapped	Rev. Rul. 70-395, 1970-2 CB 65
Prosthesis	Reg. § 1.213-1(e)(1)(iii)
Psychiatric care	Rev. Rul. 55-261, 1955-1 CB 307
Psychologists	Rev. Rul. 63-91, 1963-1 CB 54
Psychotherapists	Rev. Rul. 63-91, 1963-1 CB 54
Reclining chair for cardiac patient	Rev. Rul. 58-155, 1958-1 CB 156
Reconstructive surgery, breast	Rev. Rul. 2003-57, 2003-1 CB 959
Remedial reading for dyslexic children	Rev. Rul. 69-607, 1969-2 CB 40
Retirement home, cost of medical care	H.W. Smith Est., 79 TC 313, Dec. 39,273 (Acq.)
Sanitarium rest home, cost of, medical, educational, or rehabilitative reasons	Reg. § 1.213-1(e)(1)(v)
Schools, special, relief of handicap	Rev. Rul. 58-533, 1958-2 CB 108; Rev. Rul. 69-499, 1969-2 CB 39; Rev. Rul. 70-285, 1970-1 Cb52
Service animals - hearing-aid animal - other - seeing-eye dog	 Rev. Rul.68-295, 1968-1 CB 92 Senate Finance Committee Report to P.L. 100-647 Rev. Rul. 55-261, 1955-1 CB 307
Sexual dysfunction, treatment for	Rev. Rul. 75-187, 1975-1 CB 92
Smoking, program to stop	Rev. Rul. 99-28, 1999-1 CB 1269

© 2004 - 2016 Asset Protection Services of America. All Rights Reserved. AssetProtectionServices.com

Medical Expense Deductions	Revenue Ruling / Code Section / Regulation
Sterilization operation, legal	Rev. Rul. 73-603, 1973-2 CB 76, clarifying Rev. Rul. 73-201, 1973-1 CB 140
Swimming pool, treatment of polio or arthritis	C.B. Mason, DC Hawaii, 57-2 USTC ¶ 10,012; Rev. Rul. 83-33, 1983-1 CB 70
Taxicab to doctor's office	Rev. Rul. 55-261, 1955-1 CB 307
Teeth, artificial	Reg. § 1.213-1(e)(1)(ii)
Telephone, specially equipped - deaf persons - modified for person in an iron lung	Rev. Rul.71-48, 1971-1 CB 99, amplified by Rev. Rul. 73-53, 1973-1 CB 139 Rev. Rul. 55-261, 1955-1 CB 307
Television, closed caption decoder	Rev. Rul. 80-340, 1980-2 CB 81
Transplant, donor's costs of	Rev. Rul. 68-452, 1968-2 CB 111; Rev. Rul. 73-189, 1973-1 CB 139
Transportation, cost incurred essentially and primarily for medical care	Code Sec. 213(d)(1)(B) and Reg. § 1.213-1 (e)(1)(iv)
Vasectomy, legal	Rev. Rul. 73-201, 1973-1 CB 140, clarified by Rev. Rul. 73-603, 1973-2 CB 76, and Rev. Rul. 97-9, 1997-1 CB 77
Visual alert system for hearing impaired	IRS Letter Ruling 8250040, 9-13-82, CCH IRS Letter Ruling Reports
Weight loss program for treatment of specific disease	Rev. Rul. 2002-19, 2002-1 CB 778
Wheelchair	Reg. § 1.213-1(e)(1)(iii)
Wig (alleviation of mental discomfort resulting from disease)	Rev. Rul. 62-189, 1962-2 CB 88
X-rays	Reg. § 1.213-1(e)(1)(ii)

© 2004 - 2016 Asset Protection Services of America. All Rights Reserved. AssetProtectionServices.com

www.ingramcontent.com/pod-product-compliance
Lightning Source LLC
Chambersburg PA
CBHW052055190326
41519CB00002BA/234